Also by Len Baynes

Subby and the Undersea World

THOUGHTS OF ME

By

Len Baynes

Spinetinglers Publishing
www.spinetinglerspublishing.com

Spinetinglers Publishing
22 Vestry Road, Co. Down
BT23 6HJ, UK
www.spinetinglerspublishing.com

First published by Spinetinglers Publishing
1st October 2009.

ISBN: 978-1-906755-04-1

Printed in the United Kingdom

TO MY GRANDAUGHTER "RISSA"

TABLE OF CONTENTS

HERO'S SONG

So peacefully sleep the heroes of
    England's Greatest hour,
They rode the seas,
They flew the skies,
They fought the desert sand,
Their lives they gave with honour
To preserve this gracious land.

So listen to all their whispers
As their spirits float the skies,
Did they give their lives for nothing,
Would tears now bedim their eyes?
When they see the world in anguish
Could they really then believe
That they gave their lives as heroes
Just to watch as we deceive?

Len Baynes

Come now, if you remember,
Tell those who did not see
Of the many lives uncounted,
Lost, so that now we could be free.
They take it all for granted,
All the deeds that then were done,
Had they been on the fields of valour,
Ask still, "Would we have won?"

So blessed be the heroes
As peacefully they lie,
In fields forever England,
O'er in freedom we pass by.
Now roll the drums in honour,
And lift their banner high,
Be proud of all your heroes,
In thoughts, they'll never die.

WHISPERS IN THE WIND

We are the whispering of the wind,
The crying of the rain,
The softly falling snowflakes,
Upon the vast and open plain.

We are the mighty mountains,
Stately that reach a star kissed sky,
The rolling heaving restless sea,
O'er which our spirits fly.

Therefore, heed our cries, O mortal man,
Lay down your greed and lust.
For we have lived a million years,
And know in what to trust.

Len Baynes

But you have lived a speck of time,
And take the world as yours,
But we will last beyond your prime,
Beyond all man made laws.

So hear the whispering of the wind,
The crying of the rain,
That we may live a million years,
With you in peace again.

FRIENDSHIP

I was down, and you were there,
A beacon, through my dark despair,
That crushed me as the darkest cloud,
And had me crying out aloud
Come Help Me!!

Now the cloud has lifted high,
My thoughts and mind in freedom fly.
No more the black abyss around,
A friendship's light I have found
Of tears and blackness I am free,
As a friend indeed,
You came and you Helped Me!!

THOUGHTS OF MY DREAM

In my mind, on the wings of dreams,
A face appears, a face that seems
To take my mind, my heart, my life,
An angel face to calm the strife
Of weary days.

This face appears with thoughts of you,
The love you give comes shining through,
Those weary days just disappear
When you, my love, are near.

So come to me and share my life,
The love you give, I give,
The love I give, accept,
Then as one, we'll face the passing days,
Safe in the strength of a love that stays
Forever.

WORLD OF A CHILD

Pray, take the young child by the hand,
And tell him "Child, this is your land."
The sea, the sky, the mountains high,
The forest green, and the winds that sigh
Thro' trees that stand like banners furled
And say "Look, child this is the World."

Notice, not the crimes that we have done,
The things we've killed, then just for fun.
The ravages we've wreaked upon this
   earth,
All the beasts we've slain before your
   birth.

But see it, as we try to show,
The world before our crimes dragged low
The beauty that once was ours,
The tall green trees that shaded flowers,
In peaceful valleys 'neath mountains
  high,
With crystal clear streams cascading by.

But now, we've spoiled most everything
So tell us, "stop," then you can bring
A love of things that once were free,
A future bright that you can see,
A world that once was very grand.
Then tell us, "Go, this is our land."

SOLITUDE

I sit 'neath the glow of the night stars
   charm,
A mind at ease with body calm.
Surveying the dreams, in which I bless,
The rolling plains of emptiness.
The sea, the sky, the desert sand,
I wish for a secret place, in a secret land.
But man has tamed the sea, the plain,
The desert soon will bloom again.
Will man find my secret land, but no,
For I alone possess,
The secrets of that emptiness.

LOVE SONG

The love of my life
Is the light of my life
The light of my life is you.
The dream of my life,
Through the whole of my life,
Is to spend all my life with you.

So, come tell me now
That the dreams of my life,
That the dreams of my life may soon
    come true,
And then I may spend all the days of my
    life
In happiness with you.

THE EYES OF A CHILD

The world of a child is a sight to see,
Come let me help you, come share it with
   me.
All the colours of the rainbow, so
   wonderfully bright,
Through the eyes of a child,
A kaleidoscope of light.
All things are mystery, no one is foe,
Friends and fun times, wherever you go.
No one is evil, nothing is wrong,
The whole world is covered with a child's
   happy song.

That old piece of wood is a jungle tree,
That little black cat, a panther you see.
All life's an adventure, but time passes
    fast,
And all that is seen can never last.
Give me forever the eyes of a child,
Let me see all things, all people pleasant
    and mild.
But stay, not at me, bring in the whole
    world,
Let the joy that is seen,
Be a banner unfurled.
Then all the things that man has defiled,
Would not be there
Through the eyes of a child.

SONG OF THE TALL SHIPS

I gaze at a picture of a graceful ship,
Sailing on a storm tossed sea,
I gaze at that picture,
And I see that ship, I see that ship as me.

At times I pass 'neath the southern cross,
Under starlit tropic sky,
And thence with trade winds roaring full,
Like an albatross I fly.

From north to south, from east to west,
I'd traverse oceans all
Under leaden skies, on rolling seas,
Where the seabirds plaintiff call.

With Cutty Sark, Thermopylae,
Great ships so stately tall,
We cross the oceans of the world,
Through voyage to landfall.

But now have gone,
Titania, Flying Cross, Taeping,
All wondrous ships of a bygone age,
Whose history I sing.

No more to bend to wind, wild free,
Flying onward, onward cross endless sea,
Where the great whale sounds,
And the seabirds cry,
And the tall, tall ships pierce the ocean's
    sky.

And so I sat and reminisced,
On a bygone age my life has missed,
I see that picture, and I dream aloud,
Cross the wild free sea,
Board the flying cloud.

I need to climb a mountain
I need to reach the stars,
I need to find the secrets,
Of Jupiter and Mars.

But I am but a mortal man
And I can hope to see,
The secrets of the Universe,
Or are they locked forever
From mere mortals such as me.

MY LADY

Chill is the early morning air,
The dawn's grey light is creeping,
Through the curtains of my hearts
    despair,
Whilst my lady lies a sleeping.

The hours drag through this lonely night,
A sleepless watch I'm keeping,
The day will pass to fading light,
Whilst my lady lies a sleeping.

I could sleep a peaceful sleep,
No dark thoughts to mind a leaping,
If I could be a lying there,
Where my lady is a sleeping.

But there is no way that I could stay,
With my love a dreaming,
There is another lying there,
Where my lady lies a sleeping.

So yet again I hope in vain,
My lonely watch still keeping,
The love I have just brings me pain,
Whilst my lady lies a sleeping.

FREEDOM

I see a tall and stately ship
Upon a restless sea,
My mind could be that graceful ship,
That the wind is blowing free.

Above my ship, a graceful bird
Soars through the clouds on high,
Again my mind could be that bird,
With freedom yet to fly.

The crashing waves that ever smash
The rocks of earthly grime,
Are oft times peaceful and serene,
Still flee through endless time.

My mind can span that ageless time
And see again my ship,
And in my bird that soars on high
Across the highest mountains,
With peaks that reach the sky,
My mind can timeless wander,
And in freedom, every fly.

In the realm of make believe,
Where children and the young at heart
    perceive,
A Land so full of our old friends.
Down the yellow brick rod and round the
    bends.
We'll see them all just waiting there
So don't hang back, don't stand and stare.
Here's Alice, White Rabbit too
And there's the Old Lady in her shoe,
Tinkerbell and Peter Pan,
Cowardly Lion with Tin man.
Toad is racing down a hole,
Chased by Ratty and the Mole.
Elves and Goblins, Fairies too,
Wait in this land of dreams for you.

As the daylight needs the morning sun
And the night a moon that's true.
As the oceans need the rivers run,
Then darling I need you.

Think not of times before we met,
The times of troubled strife.
But think of years we've yet to come,
I'll dedicate my life.

So please come to me as you have,
In the years past,
And know that I will promise you,
A love to ever last.

The foresails full,
The spinnaker high.
The mainsail call is full and bye.
Beneath the Southern Cross we fly.
Onward, onward, the wind draws free,
Across the world come back for me.

Then take my mind as the sea birds fly,
Above restless sea cross-endless sky.
The foresails full.
The spinnaker High.
The mainsail call is full and bye.

I wish again to see my life
And note the things I've done.
The many things that I regret
And those just done in fun.
To sail again the endless sea,
That ever calls me now.
To find again the friends I've lost
And not to wonder how.
But now my life is winding down,
These things are long gone past
The happiness I need I've found
And peace is mind at last.

The sea so wild so restless free,
Then calm to soothe the anguished soul.
It crashes on some foreign shore,
Then rolls back to me, to show me more.

The sky above so azure blue,
Will sparkle in a sunset's hue.
Then darken black with thunders roar,
Can change again to show me more.

The mountains tall reach a star filled
    sky,
A mighty eagle gives a strident cry.
All life will give to nature's law
And that's my God, that shows me more.

So talk not to me of man made Gods,
Through unknown fears conceive
And ancient fabled stories told,
In Koran, Bible, Hebrew scrolls, that I
    cannot believe.

But listen to the ancient ones,
Now so long time dead.
And heed the wisdom you will find,
In the words that they have said.

The sea, the sky, the mountains high,
The restless wind still whispers by.
So look to nature, tell all mankind,
They are the Gods that you should find.

WHY?

High in the heavens, where angels fly,
A soldier's spirit drifting by, was asked
  by a mother,
"Where and why, did my only son have to
  die?"
The spirit turned and gently said,
"In which great battle did he tread?
I've seen them all o'er countless years,
I've seen the fields where poppies bled.
Their scarlet profusion over countless
  dead.
I've seen the tanks in desert sand
Spitting their death at a mortal band,
I've lay in trenches, when shells, Round
  after round
Have mangled men and churned the
  ground.
I've known them all who died this way
Over all this time, day by endless day.
So gentle mother dry your tear,
Your son I know is very near.

But why he died, I have no answer, to
 that I fear."
The spirit cradled the mother's head
And led her to where her son lay dead.
And still she sits as the years pass by,
Softly asking "Why, oh Why?"

THE STORM

The grey sky hails the rising dawn
But darker now, it does forewarn
Of things to come.
The breeze that stirred with gentle kiss
Begins to sing a Devils tryst
And warns of things to come
Darker now the clouds that hide the sun
No more the sea with sheen of glass
More restless waves have seen that pass.
The deck beneath my feet is lively now
The gentle breeze its voice begins to howl
Through shrouds aglow with Elmo's fire
As waves once slight, grow higher, higher
The rumbling sound of distant thunder
The lightning's flash, shows the clouds
   asunder
And nature's wrath begins to plunder
The hearts of men
Stinging rain, and howling wind,
Lightning flash, and thunder roar
She dips, she rolls, she staggers more

~And men aboard now crave the shore.
A wicked, reeling beam end roll
A crashing sea, that bears the soul
Of frightened men.
Then slightly but perceptively grew light
Invades the leaden sky
The shrieking, howling banshee wind
Becomes a gentle sigh.
The heaving, rolling, yawning deck
Is quieter, more stable now
And moves through gently rolling sea
With noble elegant bow.
The remnant sails on topmast yard that
    sang with whip like crack
Are hanging with abated noise
Silently and slack.
So man the yards, bend on new sail
We've no more seas to roam
And then this ship, this tall, tall ship,
Heels to the wind for home.

Daylight fades, no more the sun
The long dark lonely hours
Again the battles won.
We stand alone 'gainst horrors hosts
Who won the day?
Was it just few years ago
In youthful pride we stood

To cleanse the world corrupted so
They told us yes
We knew we could
When did the glory and the honour fade?
When did the carnage first invade?
Was it in some far off field
When grim reaper darked the sun?
And thousands knew the hell
The nightmare had begun
So tell the young who haven't seen
The terrors that we've known
That when they see the evil wrought
The seeds of peace are sown.

So long the night as darkness hides the
    dawn
And night time's sounds hold back the
    birth of morn
The twilight brings a consciousness of
    mind
That makes a peaceful sleep so hard to
    find
I sit alone through shadows of my world
While all around do sleep with dreams
    unfurled
A wakeful mind from which I wish to flee
To peaceful sleep again denied to me
Here comes the first grey light of day

And banished now the darkness that held
  sway
O'er all the hours my thoughts have
  wished away.

I've trod the path, the path to hell,
The way beset by demons.
I've seen the black abyss so well,
The way directs the demons.

Then came the light, a shining light,
The lady was my sorrow.
The love I had, if the demons go
The lady's my tomorrow.

No more to see the black, black night,
The deep abyss no more in sight.
The demons even put to flight,
For this my lady,
Thank you.

LOVE OF LIFE

The love of life
Is a graceful bird
Soaring through the evening sky.
The love of life
Is a snow-cap peak
Of a grandiose mountain high.

The love of life
Is a valley serene
With nature's calm,
Where the beasts of the fields may
   wander,
Knowing nought of harm.

The love of life
Is a child's smile
Innocent and clean,
The love of life
Is mother, the child smile ever seen.

The love of life
Is a searching mind
With freedom yet to roam,
The love of life
Is a quiet time
In the peace of a place called home.

And though we may ever ponder
On the troubles of mankind
If time and thought for all, we gave,
The love of life we'd find.

HEART OF A CHILD

Your children are not children for long
Their lives all too quickly move on
So enjoy while you may, every God given
    day
Before your child's childhood years have
    gone.

Think of all the times, long gone by
Many times, maybe laugh, maybe cry
At things they have done albeit in fun
Remember and wistfully sigh.

Know not of anger, or pain
That childhood days cannot come back
    again
Remember with joy, be it girl, be it boy
But children they cannot remain.

Just help them through life all you can
And when that child that you had, is a
   man
You will see when he lovingly smiles
That you still own the heart of a child.

WHY OH WHY

So many days have passed me by
So many days to still ask why?
Why the sun in heavens high
And why the moon as night drawn nigh?

Are all my questions lost
In a sky of twinkling stars
Or will I ever get to know
The why of Jupiter and Mars?

Does the answer lie in a silent God
The invention of long passed time
Or was it an instants mighty blast
Can to know be such a crime?

In time to come when man has made
A stairway to the stars, and the heavens
    his new domain
Will the clouds be gone and all be clear
Or will the mystery remain?

THE GREEN FIELDS OF ENGLAND

Let me wander forever the green fields of
   England
Let me bask in the glory of its great
   bygone days.
Let me sing all the praise to the green
   fields of England,
As proudly I'd stand, its banner to raise.

Let me tell of the heroes of the green
   fields of England,
So history will know of the deeds they
   have done,
They taught the way of the green fields of
   England,
Its justice, its laws, forever to run.

Len Baynes

So teach the young child of the green
    fields of England,
When they stood alone 'gainst the world
    and its hell,
Of the lives laid down for the green fields
    of England
So we may be here, their story to tell.

So come all the young of the green fields
    of England,
Be proud of the land wherein you do
    dwell,
The future is yours, and the green fields
    of England,
Will go on forever and your stories will
    tell.

PUB TIME

A brass bound clock on a panelled wall,
A smoke stained ceiling, not so tall,
Three pictures, scenes of times gone by,
'Neath shaded lights, not very high.

The buzz of chat that's fills the air,
Contented people at the bar, just there,
No blaring noise or lights that glare
From strident machines, placed
    anywhere,
This is a pub.

You'll meet all kinds of folk in there
All kinds of folk, with whom to share
A chat, a yarn, a joke or two,
Or even a chance to air your view.

Mine host will serve what e'er you wish,
A beer, a wine, a tasty dish,
It's a world apart from worldly care,
Troubles unknown, and who would dare
To even think, and state "Revamp",
This pub, the Quiz teams know as
    CHAMP.

ENIGMA

Sometimes I sit and ponder
And often wonder why,
I cannot be as other men,
I need to go where the free birds fly.

To see the sights at the end of the world,
The realm of the Great While Whale,
To move forever on a sea of storms,
Where my dreams forever sail.

I need no daily wanderings
Through earthbound toils and woes,
My mind a free blithe spirit
That flows where the river flows.

Cross the snow-cap mountains,
With peaks that pierce the sky,
I'd touch the moon, and reach the star
In my soul, a need to fly.

Len Baynes

But now my time is waning,
And life is fleeting by,
Yet still the urge to wander
Throughout the endless sky.
I'll leave the world to other men
For this freedom can never die.

LONDON MEMORIES

From the deep recess of memory
Came the visions of my childhood,
Came the scenes of London's river
See the Banks on which we stood
To watch the ships forever passing,
And the times we had were good.

Came the times of warfare's terror
Came the night when bombs reigned
  down,
Hear the cries of dying children,
See the blasted shattered ground.
Still the nightmare dreams abound me
Pray that peace may set us free.

Len Baynes

Now in memory wartime's ended,
Great the joyous singing crowd,
Great the street held children's parties
With the music ringing loud.
But the visions tinged with sorrow
For all our friends, departed, lost
Will there be a free tomorrow
And will we ever count the cost?

Once again recall is changing,
Left behind the grimy friendly street,
Now for me the country's calling,
Fields and rivers, new friends to meet.
But in memory ever lingers
Thoughts of London's East End folk,
Sights and sounds of London's river,
Friendships made and never broke.

Now my lifespan's end is nearing
Memories cloudy, visions blurred,
Happy in peace, the time is passing
Yet still my thoughts are stirred
Of the banks of London's river
Sights and sounds and where we stood,
Memories in my mind are flowing,
Of this child, and its childhood.

STROLLING

Just take the time to wander
Down a green strewn lane, in Spring,
Hear a lark's call gently echo
As to a budded bough he's cling.

It's just a lane to England,
A long meadow's butterfly filled,
Cross peaceful stream meandering
Neath bird's nest, young to yield.

And as you quietly amble,
Under blue with white cloud sky.
You'll hear a herdsman calling
To a flock that's grazing by.

Can you see the picture changing?
As the river's gliding by,
Sit and watch the fishermen
Their peaceful sport to ply.

Enjoy this calming magic
That's there for all to know
If they would only trouble
To find the time and go.

Now hear the church bell tolling
The passing of the day
As twilight slowly falling
It's time to stroll away.

COLOURS

A black man and a white man had fought
   that day
As they both lay there dying, the crowd
   moved away
Save one small child who, thoughtfully
   said,
"Look, everybody, both bloods are red".

"Yes", said the old man, from the
   shadows nearby,
"Yes", said the old man, with a long
   drawn out sigh.
"It should trouble you not, child, the
   colour of skin,
You should look ever deeper for the man
   that's within".

"Some black men are good, some white
 men are bad,
'Tis' the way of the world that makes me
 so sad.
So, child ever think of the man you would
 find,
And thoughts of his colour leave far
 behind".

Then with a smile, he turned 'neath the
 light,
One half of him black, the other half
 white.

WONDERING

I sit and gaze at a starlit sky,
A gossamer cloud goes floating by,
And I wonder.

I sit beside a still calm sea,
With nought in the world
Save the sea and me,
And I wonder.

When the storm clouds clash
On the mountains high,
And lightning rends a turbulent sky,
Nature's wrath is running free,
Where in this world is place for me?
I wonder.

Did nature's hand conceive us here?
Or in a puff of wind did we appear?
Do all our Gods really make it clear?
I wonder.

Len Baynes

When in the far and distant time,
When all we know is dust and grime,
Will somebody there still be inclined
To wonder?

READERS' NOTES

Len Baynes

Thoughts of Me

Len Baynes